FREE SOLO
CLIMBING

A free solo in Yosemite National Park, California

FREE SOLO CLIMBING

ODYSSEYS

TRACEY MILLER

CREATIVE EDUCATION · CREATIVE PAPERBACKS

Published by Creative Education and Creative Paperbacks
P.O. Box 227, Mankato, Minnesota 56002
Creative Education and Creative Paperbacks
are imprints of
The Creative Company
www.thecreativecompany.us

Design and production by Blue Design (www.bluedes.com)
Art direction by Rita Marshall
Edited by Kremena Spengler

Alamy Stock Photo/BFA, 64, Corey Rich / Aurora Photos, 56, TMI, cover, YAY Media, 24; Getty Images/Cavan Images, 6, 34–35, China News Service, 66, Education Images, 70–71, JEAN-PIERRE CLATOT, 47, Variety, 63, VW Pics, 69, Westend61, 39; Unsplash/Amy Gatenby, 75, Nicolas Weldingh, 19; Wikimedia Commons/ARG_Flickr, 12, 31, Bops92, 15, brewbooks, 4–5, Cmichel67, 59, Emmanuel Aguirre, Robi Bosh, 48, graeme. leuchars, 51, Heinz Zak, 2, Jerry moffatt1, 11, Martin Mason Hazeltine, 28, McKay Savage, 60, Medena Rosa, 20, Melgna, 8, Pat Ament, 37, public domain, 44, Nimra, 26

Library of Congress Cataloging-in-Publication Data
Names: Miller, Tracey, 1971- author.
Title: Free solo climbing / by Tracey Miller.
Description: Mankato, Minnesota : Creative Education and Creative Paperbacks, [2025] | Series: Odysseys in extreme sports | Includes bibliographical references and index. | Audience: Ages 12-15 years | Audience: Grades 7-9 | Summary: “Embark on a thrill-filled ascent with this title for high school readers about free solo climbing, the daring pursuit of scaling rock faces without ropes or harnesses. Includes skills and equipment needed, a glossary, index, and further resources”– Provided by publisher.
Identifiers: LCCN 2024030291 (print) | LCCN 2024030292 (ebook) | ISBN 9798889893103 (lib. bdg.) | ISBN 9781682776766 (paperback) | ISBN 9798889894216 (ebook)
Subjects: LCSH: Free solo climbing–Juvenile literature.
Classification: LCC GV200.25 .M55 2025 (print) | LCC GV200.25 (ebook) | DDC 796.522–dc23/eng/20240815
LC record available at https://lccn.loc.gov/2024030291
LC ebook record available at https://lccn.loc.gov/2024030292

Printed in China

Free soloing in Joshua Tree National Park, California

A free solo climber on a vertical wall

CONTENTS

Introduction

People face many challenges every day. Challenges are simply a part of life. But some people look for challenges beyond the expected—extreme challenges. Those who seek thrills may see a massive mountain looming in the distance and get an undeniable compulsion to go to that mountain.

OPPOSITE: A view of El Capitan in Yosemite National Park in California in 2017

They may stand at the base of that huge hunk of rock, look up, and think to themselves, "This is my calling. This is something I want to give myself over to completely. I want to start here at the base, small and in the shadow of a huge force of nature, and make my way up, bit by bit, until I can stand mighty and strong, hands held high, at the top."

For those seeing a mountain for the first time, the moment can be awe-inspiring. Mountains are grand and varied, each one unique in its color, texture, height, and

Jerry Moffatt free soloing at Curbar Edge, England, United Kingdom

OPPOSITE A free solo climber in Wales, United Kingdom

width. Mountains are such mammoth creations that they can even create their own weather! They inspire quotes, and we use them as imagery when speaking of testing our limits or accomplishing monumental achievements. Actor Sylvester Stallone once said, "If you don't have a mountain, build one and then climb it. And, after you climb it, build another one; otherwise you start to flatline in your life."

The Majesty of a Mountain

Scientists usually define a mountain as a terrain that rises at least 2,000 feet (610 meters) above the surrounding area. They will tell you that many mountains are formed when **tectonic plates** move below the Earth's surface. Where these rocky tops formed, dreams of conquering them were also born. Humans are nothing if not curious, and the mountains were a quest to be completed.

OPPOSITE: Pordoi Pass in the Dolomite Mountains, Italy

There are at least five types of mountains on Earth. One type is a mountain of accumulation—or a volcanic mountain. Volcanic mountains are formed by volcanoes which erupted, piling up volcanic material over time. A second type is the fold mountain, which comes about with the collision of tectonic plates. A third kind is the mountain of erosion, which occurs when rocks wear away. A fourth kind is the dome mountain, which is created when flat-lying **sedimentary** rocks are bowed or warped, forming a dome. A fifth type is the **fault-block** mountain, which is caused by fractures in the surface of the earth.

While we have learned about how mountains came to be, we are not certain when people began to climb them for fun. Humans have been living in the mountains throughout history, however. Roughly 25 percent of the

Earth is covered in mountains, so it's no wonder that people throughout history have decided the mountains were worth climbing!

Humans have not always climbed for sport. For much of history, they have climbed out of necessity. Some climbed to survey their surroundings, identify property lines, or picture the ideal positioning for a battle. Some climbed to build altars to their gods or to see if locations rumored to be haunted actually were. Often, people simply wanted to learn about the world around them, especially to conduct **meteorological** and **geological** studies, as well as botanical and geographical research.

Mountain climbing sparked a fierce desire in some to see what they could achieve when pitted against Mother Nature. In 1786, Swiss scientist Horace Bénédict de Saussure organized a successful contest to climb to the top of Mont Blanc in the French Alps. He had attempted to climb it himself, but, upon his own failure, decided to challenge others to reach the summit by offering a reward. It was the first time

Mountains Make Weather

Mountains create their own weather. They alter the path of the wind, sheltering some areas and making others windy. When humid ocean air hits a mountain, it is forced to rise. The air then cools and expands, creating clouds. The clouds make rain or snow, helping things grow on that side of the mountain. Mountains can also block rain from falling in the valleys, creating dry climates. If you take a road trip along the Alaska Highway (known as Al-Can) which runs from Canada to Alaska, you could experience bright sunshine a few miles from a mountain and, upon approaching the mountain, you might find snow or rain.

Nature's Free Solo Climbers

Mountain goats are thought to be the best climbers—even better than the most skilled humans. These animals' hooves have two toes that spread out and act as built-in tools which give them a wide, sturdy base for each step. Mountain goats use their hooves to grab onto rocks the way humans use their fingers. The animals also have hard pads on their feet that make them less likely to slip. When they push off, their front legs stay close to their body and their back legs spread out. Their strong shoulders help them climb and dig through snow in winter to find food.

in recorded history that climbing was seen as a sport. Many climbers tried, but it took 25 years for a climber to claim the prize. The effort sparked a great interest in mountain climbing by **alpinists** across the continent of Europe, including Saussure, who eventually made the trek as well.

In the 1950s, many people sought to scale the Himalayan mountains in Asia. Mountain climbers from many countries claimed victory over the ranges that stretch across the northeastern portion of India, but New Zealander Sir Edmund Hillary and his Tibetan guide

Tenzing Norgay were the first to successfully reach the top of Mount Everest, the tallest peak on Earth, in 1953.

Hillary had always been an outdoorsman. He enjoyed things like beekeeping and a holistic approach to life. The mountains just seemed to call to him. His first expedition up into the clouds was at the age of 20 when he climbed Mount Ollivier in New Zealand's Southern Alps. In 1951, Hillary joined a British expedition to Everest.

Norgay had plenty of experience in the mountains. He had been involved in almost every attempt to climb

Everest, setting records along the way. So, the two teamed up and, using the knowledge of the previous climbs and some extra oxygen, they found themselves making history as the first to climb to the highest point on Earth.

In the 1960s, the sport of climbing began to change. Great heights had been reached, and the new challenge became finding more difficult routes into the same mountains. Climbing tools and techniques allowed alpinists to scale smooth rock faces as well. The history of mountain climbing was just beginning.

The Freedom of Free Solo Climbing

During the time of Hillary and Norgay—and into the 1970s—nylon rope was vital to mountain climbing. This material was stronger and safer than the previously used Manila hemp rope (made from a plant that grows in the Philippines). Swami belts—harnesses containing holsters for tools such as **piton** hammers—were first worn during this time. Climbers relied on the harnesses and very strong woven nylon called webbing. They also used carabiners—D-shaped clips made of steel—to hold gear together.

OPPOSITE: A free solo climber is outlined against the sky at sunset.

Mountain climbing equipment

The older tools were relatively heavy and cumbersome, but they kept evolving. Over time, manufacturers began to replace the steel tools with a lighter alternative—aluminum. The number of tools was reduced, so that the process could be streamlined. But there were still many things needed to outfit each climber—climbing shoes, **dynamic** and **static ropes**, various carabiner clips, hooks, helmets, harnesses, **crampons**, ice axes, and **belay** and **rappelling** devices.

Another important tool developed at this time was the system of grading called the Yosemite

South Dome from Glacier Point.

The Yosemite Decimal System

The Yosemite Decimal System is used mostly in the United States. The first number in each grade relates to "class," with 1 being relatively flat terrain and 5 being a rock wall for which any climb would require the use of special gear. The second part refers to the difficulty of the climb. The range is from 2 to 15 based on how hard the maneuvers will be and how big the holds are along the route. The letter at the end of the grade—a, b, c, or d—gives more specificity to the difficulty a climber will encounter. Another system—the French Grading Scale, also known as the Fontainebleau Scale—is used mostly outside the U.S.

Decimal System. This system was developed so that the climbers would understand the difficulty of the routes they were climbing. The bigger the number, the more difficult the climb. The rating is subjective, as the grade is given by the first person to climb it. That grade can be challenged by those who climb after. If the route changes due to weather or an avalanche, for example, there may be a debate to reassess the grade assigned.

As evolved as the tools of the trade were, free solo climbing effectively wiped the slate clean in the 1970s, by taking all of the tools away and bringing climbers to a whole new level of tool—the climber's own body. He or she relied solely on their feet and fingers to climb steep and **technical** rock faces. The only potential enhancement to these well-conditioned fingers and toes was a pair of climbing shoes to grip the slick faces of the mountains and a bag of chalk to keep the fingers dry.

Picture a speck of a person, just a spot of bright color moving along the slick face of a mountain. That spot of color would be making steady progress, finding tiny cracks, **crevices**, and subtle ledges to grip with their fingers and toes. Take a closer look. That bright speck has no rope or glint of crampons on their climbing boots. There is nothing to keep them tethered to the broad face of the enormous mountain. It is normal in any sporting event to witness great feats of strength in an athlete, but in extreme sports such as mountain climbing or free soloing, there is a shiver up the neck of the observer and a tickle in the tummy at what they're witnessing. Free soloing just might evoke the biggest shiver and the craziest tickle.

Free soloing is considered an incredibly dangerous sport, even in the arena of extreme sports. The number of climbers who set their sights on this type of challenge is tiny, and many have died trying. Some recent studies put the number of free soloing deaths at about 30 a year.

A free solo climber in Wales, United Kingdom

Forty-three percent of the fatalities were due to falls, 34 percent were due to avalanches, and 23 percent were from heart attacks or other causes..

Soloing is an exercise of the mind, body, and spirit. A person cannot simply go into the sport of free soloing without legs that could carry them and arms that could hold them in place on the side of the rock face—not to mention a mind that believes it can achieve such a lofty goal.

When it comes to the mind, some climbers meditate or pray. Some free solo climbers won't allow cameras to film them or photographs to be taken as they climb. They keep their climbing life completely private, unwilling to speak about it publicly. Some say the mindset they develop in climbing affects their entire lives. This is the most physical game of chess and the most demanding mental puzzle, all in the form of a sport.

For the body, being fit is essential. Some will do yoga, stretching the body, or "hang," which is an exercise for the fingers. The preparation of the body is intense. Breathing in high altitudes also requires practice and preparation. The climbs take place in all sorts of weather and in all types of temperatures. The body must be ready for these factors, as well.

A young man climbs a vertical rock without any equipment.

Those Who Came Before

The history of free solo climbing is filled with fascinating people who made treacherous climbs. One of the world's first free soloists was John Bachar. He was nicknamed "Mr. Norelco" after a popular cordless electric razor. Bachar was likewise "cordless"—unencumbered by any climbing gear. Bachar began to climb in his teen years and made a name for himself in the climbing community by free soloing three very challenging routes on the 450-foot (137-meter) Nabisco Wall in Yosemite National Park in California.

OPPOSITE: John Bachar

Yosemite is a place many climbers seek out, and 19-year-old Henry Barber was no different. Barber was visiting Yosemite and saw a rock face called Steck-Salathe. Then and there, he decided he would free solo its 1,500-foot (457-meter) surface. He had never seen, much less climbed, this route, and he did it successfully in only 2.5 hours! Three years later, Barber soloed the Strand in North Wales in the United Kingdom "on sight," or having never studied or climbed it, with a television show called *The American Sportsman* filming him. During this arduous ascent, Barber's hat was stolen by a seagull passing by, as the climber scaled above the beautiful waters of the Atlantic Ocean. All in all throughout his lifetime of climbing, 87 percent of Barber's free soloing climbs were on sight.

In the 1970s and the 1980s, Earl Wiggins, a Colorado native, climbed many difficult free solo routes. He is

Ladies Climb, Too

The Ladies Alpine Club was founded in Britain in 1907. The men's climbing club, the Alpine Club of Great Britain, would not allow women to be members, so they formed their own oganization. In 1974, a vote was taken to merge the two clubs, but it failed. In 1975, the vote passed so that the men's and women's climbing clubs could combine, but even then some of the members saw the merger as controversial.

known for having fallen 30 feet (9 m) off of Outer Limits, a route in Yosemite, surviving and returning to climb it successfully at a later date. His career as a Hollywood **rigger** may have been what led him to seek the thrill of climbing mountains.

While the 1970s brought a strong lineup of free solo climbers, the 1980s did not disappoint. Peter Croft was the first to free solo the Rostrum, which is 4,616 feet (1,407 m) tall, and Astroman, which is 1,000 feet (305 m) tall, both in

Yosemite. That wasn't enough for Croft. He later soloed both of these routes in one day.

Austin Howell was a climber whose trademark was a grey newsboy cap. One day in 2015, Howell's climb up Dopey Duck in Linville Gorge in North Carolina was being filmed, when the camera crew realized he was naked except for that cap. A closeup of the man also revealed he didn't have shoes on. Howell was known to be a carefree climbing rebel. He shared his feelings on climbing by saying, "Free soloing isn't a death wish, it's a life wish. It's the single best therapy I've ever found for calming my tumultuous mind. The control that I've developed on the wall transfers into my daily life."

Clark Jacobs loved one particular route so much he climbed it 500 times. This trail, called the Flower of High Rank, is a very interesting trail in California known for having a tree growing between the north face and the northeast face. It is ranked as one of the most challenging routes in the world at a 5.9.

Women can also be counted in the history of free solo climbing. In 2007, Steph Davis became the first woman to solo the Diamond, the sheer northeast face of Longs Peak in the Rocky Mountain National Park, Colorado, which is a 14,255-foot (4,345-meter) trek. Brette Harrington is also a fearless soloist. She has a major presence in the sport,

"IN 2007, STEPH DAVIS BECAME THE FIRST WOMAN TO SOLO THE DIAMOND."

having climbed in the area of South America known as Patagonia, many of the routes in the famed Squamish climbing community in Canada, and beyond. Catherine Destivelle of France took home a world championship for competitive climbing, and the U.K. boasts Alison Hargreaves, who is best known for climbing Everest by herself and without **supplemental** oxygen.

Free soloing has variations to the climb, too. Dan Osman, who aided in the development of the Cave Rock climbing area in Nevada, participated in speed soloing, a version of free solo climbing where speed is the goal.

Steph Davis

Later, Dean Potter came up with free BASE climbing, which is a free solo climb with a parachute on the back, the only additional tool to fingers, toes, and chalk.

One of the most interesting variations of soloing came from Ueli Steck of Switzerland. Ueli's nickname was "the Swiss Machine." He didn't just climb, he speed soloed, once scaling the 5,000-foot (1,524-meter) north face of the Eiger mountain in Switzerland in just over two hours! He was only 17 when he completed the most difficult level of climbs, despite the fact that he had started climbing only five years earlier.

Speed soloing is just one variation of free soloing. Alain Robert has taken the sport to a different terrain. The French climber scales mountains and buildings alike. His urban climbing has inspired documentaries and serious buzz on social media. Robert has been dubbed "the French Spiderman" because he has climbed roughly 170 buildings in his career.

Robert got his start climbing buildings at the age of 12. In college, he was locked out of his home while his

Ueli Steck

Alain Robert

parents were not due back for hours. To remedy this predicament, he climbed seven stories and let himself in. Throughout his career, Robert faced his fear of heights, as well as crushing injuries. He also suffered from debilitating vertigo, which is a sensation of whirling and loss of balance associated particularly with looking down from a great height.

Robert has climbed an impressive list of buildings. His climbs include an illegal climb of the Empire State Building in New York City; the Golden Gate Bridge in San Francisco, California; the Eiffel Tower in Paris, France; the Sydney Opera House in Sydney, Australia; and the Burj Khalifa tower in Dubai, United Arab Emirates. The Burj Khalifa is the world's tallest structure at 2,722 feet (830 m). As any free soloist does, Robert climbs with only his hands, feet, and a little chalk. He wedges his fingers between window sills, and he steps on ledges.

This incredible athlete has been listed in the Guinness Book of World Records three times. In 2011, Robert climbed the Burj Khalifa in 6 hours, 14 minutes, and 55 seconds. In 2012, he won the title of the fastest person to climb the Torch Doha, a hotel in Doha, Qatar, solo. He climbed it in 1 hour, 33 minutes, and 47 seconds. In 2015, he was awarded the honor for the most buildings climbed.

Alain Robert climbs the Four Seasons building in Hong Kong, China.

The Art of Free Soloing

There are many fantastic stories from climbing camps around the world. Podcasts, movies, and documentaries are now built around this culture. One name well known in both the climbing world and the documentary community is Alex Honnold.

Honnold began climbing at the age of five. His parents encouraged him to excel at the sport, and by the time he was 10 years old, Honnold was climbing regularly and winning climbing competitions on a local and national level. As an adult, the mountains called to him more than any other thing in his life, and he answered the call by committing to them in a big way. In 2007, he moved into a minivan and later a tent, traveling around his home state of California to pursue climbing full time. Climbing consumed his thoughts, and his every action reflected his passion for free soloing.

Honnold was well known among his climbing peers, but his fame among the general community erupted after the release of a documentary about his life. Created by Elizabeth Chai Vasarhelyi and Jimmy Chin in 2018, this film, *Free Solo*, tells of Honnold's focus on free soloing the 3,000-foot (914-meter) vertical rock El Capitan in Yosemite. His whole life was put under a microscope as he prepared to solo, which he did entirely while living in his van. It took Honnold eight years to finalize his preparations for the climb. By June 2017, Honnold had more than earned the title of the first person to free solo El Capitan, and the world paid attention.

Unlike those who climb a rock face at first sight, Honnold was a firm supporter of preparing for climbs. He journaled extensively, making notes about climbs. He made 40–50 practice runs in preparation, learning every bit of the path and how he wanted to handle every move. He became a vegetarian in an effort to become more physically lean. He lived within the shadow of El Capitan, learning his "opponent" so thoroughly that when a rock climbing arena in London recreated the hardest parts of his route up El Capitan, Honnold was able to correct their rendition from memory. The climber knew every single finger hold, every nook and cranny of the rock face, and exactly what his muscles and mind needed to do to complete the task at hand.

Video footage in the film shows the viewer just how incredible the mind and body must be to perform such an act—hanging from a rock face while the trees below appear doll-sized and the mountain itself is merely a toy that the freckle of the climber is moving along.

Alex Honnold solos the nose on El Capítan.

When it came time to actually solo El Capitan, Honnold became hyperaware of his beginning mark. He didn't want any false starts, and his instincts became his biggest tool to decide if "today was the day."

As Honnold began his big day, he was exhilarated, taking the mountain route at a faster pace than he had the day before. He **traversed** the hardest section, called the Boulder Problem, with what almost appeared to be ease on the day he claimed El Capitan. His extended karate kick move was flawless, and he

“EVERY DETAIL WAS CAPTURED ON FILM AND MADE ITS WAY TO THE PUBLIC, BRINGING FREE SOLOING TO THE FOREFRONT OF THE WORLD’S MIND.”

reached the top with a huge smile and the proclamation that he was “so delighted.” He repeated this statement several times while talking to his loved ones and pacing the gorgeous top of the mountain.

Every detail was captured on film and made its way to the public, bringing free soloing to the forefront of the world’s mind. The film became so publicized and was so well received that in 2019, it won both an Academy

Honnold in 2023

Award for Best Documentary Feature and the British BAFTA for Best Documentary. In fact, *Free Solo* garnered 54 nominations from various award organizations, resulting in 31 wins. The world was paying attention to one of the most extreme sports out there and to the athletes who participated in it.

A Life Devoted to the Climb

Marc-André LeClerc was a young Canadian who lived in tents and stairwells. He kept his lifestyle simple, but his climbing was complex. He traversed rock, ice, and just about anything in between.

OPPOSITE: Squamish, British Columbia

The documentary *The Alpinist* captured who 23-year-old LeClerc was. He was a quiet person who loved living in the lush forests around his favorite haunt in Squamish, British Columbia. With giant trees for a ceiling and huge vivid fern leaves for floors, Squamish was a great place for LeClerc to practice his free soloing and mixed climbing—climbing using some tools and some free-solo methods. He was able to vary his climbs by tackling climbs that included boulders and steep, sleek rock walls.

The documentary crew who was following him started in Squamish with him and his climbing friends. LeClerc was shy about the cameras and crew and often slipped away to climb alone. In a world of video and pictures, LeClerc was a bit of a **luddite**, keeping his climbing life private. Much of the contact with him at

In a Producer's Words

While filming the documentary *Free Solo*, Jimmy Chin, Alex Honnold's friend and producer of the film, was also interviewed about the subject. "If you had a superpower and you could fly, you would probably do it, right?," said Chin. "The drive and ambition to do something that pushes you, that you love—it's hard to put that away and not use it." Chin likened solo climbing to a gymnast's floor routine, saying, "But, the floor routine is four hours long. And, every single move, every second, you have to be performing perfectly, knowing that if you make a single mistake, you would die."

A poster for the movie *The Alpinist*

the time of the filming was done through his partner Brette Harrington's phone.

People who knew LeClerc said he could "read" the weather and the mountain itself. He knew "in his gut" when it was time to climb and when it was time to hold back. Alex Honnold, who admired his fellow climber, once said of LeClerc, "His soloing wasn't about the athletic activity, it wasn't about sport. It was about a spiritual commitment to adventure."

LeClerc enjoyed a fringe version of soloing called ice climbing. He would put on his boots outfitted with crampons. These crampons allowed him to kick into the wall of ice, finding purchase. LeClerc made climbing a frozen waterfall look easy. He seemed to have no fear, even stating that climbing ice without a rope or safety gear was a "casual fun adventure."

Most ice climbers make use of ropes and tethers.

In the documentary, LeClerc was meant to climb Mount Robeson, British Columbia, accompanied by a film crew to document his ascent. Instead, he left without the knowledge of the film crew, making the climb alone. The crew was flabbergasted, but LeClerc explained he just needed to "solo" his solo. He told the film crew it just

"LECLERC SEEMED TO HAVE NO FEAR, EVEN STATING THAT CLIMBING ICE WITHOUT A ROPE OR SAFETY GEAR WAS A 'CASUAL FUN ADVENTURE.'"

hadn't felt right to do the climb with others watching. He eventually became comfortable with the pressure, and the documentary was created.

The documentary also follows a climb LeClerc made in Patagonia in 2016. He traveled there, lived with a local family, and made the first solo winter climb of a trail called Torre Egger. The same path had been climbed in

1976 by a team of Americans and again in 2010, in the first winter climb, by a group of Swiss climbers. They had ropes, harnesses, and other safety gear. LeClerc was going to do it free solo, amongst heavy ice and snow.

His first attempt was met with a blizzard. He had climbed four pitches (which means sections) of his route and found a tiny ledge on which to spend the night. At one point, he woke up to heavy snowfall and a hard decision. It was time to abandon this climb and rappel down, forfeiting his victory. The footage in the documentary of LeClerc making his descent in a blizzard is both spectacular and terrifying. He, on the other hand, seemed to take it all in stride.

A few days later, he started up Torre Egger again with a new plan in mind, saying he needed to "read the signals the mountains are sending." He successfully completed his history-making free solo climb in the beautiful mountains

Torre Egger

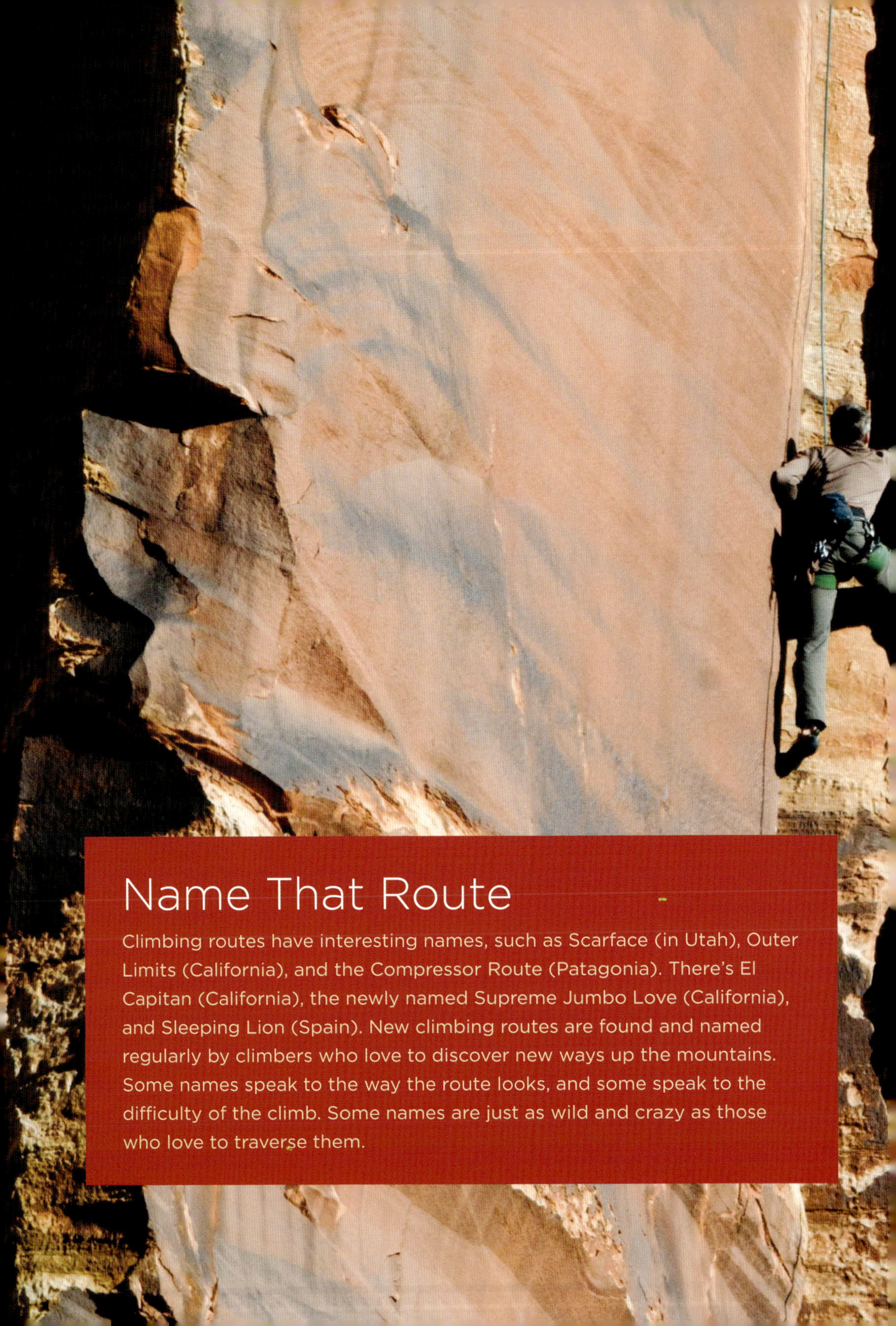

Name That Route

Climbing routes have interesting names, such as Scarface (in Utah), Outer Limits (California), and the Compressor Route (Patagonia). There's El Capitan (California), the newly named Supreme Jumbo Love (California), and Sleeping Lion (Spain). New climbing routes are found and named regularly by climbers who love to discover new ways up the mountains. Some names speak to the way the route looks, and some speak to the difficulty of the climb. Some names are just as wild and crazy as those who love to traverse them.

Scarface, Utah

of Patagonia in the dead of winter, creating a huge stir amongst his climbing peers.

After the filming of *The Alpinist* wrapped, LeClerc kept climbing. On March 5, 2018, LeClerc met with friend and fellow climber Ryan Johnson to climb Mendenhall Towers in Alaska. They planned to complete a new route up through the snow and ice. When the men's families hadn't heard from them for several days, they went to Alaska and flew over the area the men had been climbing. A hook and a bit of red rope were all that could be seen in the blinding snow. An avalanche had taken the lives of both LeClerc and Johnson.

LeClerc's peers call him a revolutionary in the world of alpinism. He simply said, "Acknowledging that your life is finite, and that it's going to end at some point, does help you lead a more intentional life, and so I think that's one of the real values. It reminds you that the rest of your time is precious, and you should use it the way that it gives you the most meaning."

Mapping, practicing, planning—these are as necessary as any tool a climber might use. Instinct tells most of us free soloing is dangerous. The free soloist just wants to climb, despite knowing the reality, following their dreams and visions. They are finding invisible toeholds and nonexistent finger ledges in the sides of mountains that even the plants struggle to cling to. They are defying gravity and defeating the doubts in their heads.

Free solo climbing will likely never be a category in the Olympics like speed climbing, **bouldering**, or **lead climbing**, but it has created an entire culture. Beyond the documentaries, there are podcasts, YouTube channels, Reddit forums, and a whole range of social media platforms featuring the sport. Maybe Alex Honnold said it best when he said, "I think that free soloing is a very emotionally charged subject, so it draws strong reactions from everybody. If you fall and die, everybody says you're an idiot, you're a risk taker, you're a daredevil... If you succeed, everybody celebrates you as a big hero. But, the reality is that you're the same person either way."

A free solo climber in Northumberland, England, United Kingdom

Selected Bibliography

Free Solo. Directed by Jimmy Chin and Elizabeth Chai Vasarhelyi. United States: National Geographic Partners, December 13, 2018.

Grey, Will. "These 10 unreal free solo climbs will wow you." Red Bull. October 23, 2017. https://www.redbull.com/us-en/10-most-epic-free-solo-climbs.

Honnold, Alex and David Roberts. *Alone on the Wall*. W. W. Norton & Company, 2018.

Smoot, Jeff. *All and Nothing: Inside Free Soloing*. Mountaineers Books, 2022.

The Alpinist. Directed by Peter Mortimer and Nick Rosen. United States: Red Bull GmbH and Sender Films, September 10, 2021.

Glossary

alpinist a mountain climber. The word comes from the Alps, a mountain range in Europe.

belay a technique in rock climbing where a climber is secured by a rope controlled by another person (known as the belayer)

bouldering rock climbing that focuses on climbing short routes close to the ground, called "problems," without ropes or harnesses

crampon a vertical steel point attached to footwear to help climb on ice

crevice a narrow opening resulting from a split or crack in a rock or cliff

dynamic rope stretchy rope used in climbing to absorb the impact of a fall

fault block a large block of rock created by tectonic stresses in Earth's crust

geological related to the study of Earth's materials, processes, and history

lead climbing climbing that involves clipping a rope attached to your harness onto bolts as you climb

luddite a person who is opposed to technological change

meteorological	related to the study of weather
piton	a steel spike hammered into a crack in a vertical wall, to provide a solid anchor for descents and ascents
rappel	lower oneself from a mountainside with a rope coiled around the body
rigger	a person who works with ropes, lifts, and hoists in a stage performance, film, or television program
sedimentary	formed by layers of material carried by water or wind and pressed together
static rope	a rope designed to stretch very little, which helps climbers control descents and haul gear
supplemental	additional
technical	requiring the development of specific physicial skills and techniques
tectonic plate	a massive, irregularly shaped slab of solid rock made up of Earth's crust and upper mantle
traverse	travel across or through

Websites

Alain ROBERT French Spiderman Inspirational Motivational Speaker...
https://www.alainrobert.com
Visit the website of free solo climber Alain Robert, nicknamed the French Spiderman.

Alpinist - The Climbing Life
https://alpinist.com/
Read features about famous climbers, including free soloists, and other information.

Climbing news mountaineering on PlanetMountain.com
https://www.planetmountain.com/en/home
Check out news about climbing and climbers, including free solo climbs and climbers.

How do mountains form
https://www.livescience.com/planet-earth/how-do-mountains-form
Learn about the types of mountains and how they were formed.

Index